SELF-HELP BOOK
OVERCOMING OBSTACLES IN DESTINY.
MARK JOHN NDAGI

OVERCOMING OBSTACLES IN DESTINY.

"Self-help Book"

Let go for resilience, goal setting, time management, and overcoming fear and self-doubt.

Mark John Ndagi

Table of content

<u>**Chapter 7: Building Resilience**</u>

- Further strategies for developing resilience
- Coping mechanisms for difficult situations

<u>**Chapter 8: Embracing Failure as a Stepping Stone**</u>

- Changing your mindset about failure
- Using failure as an opportunity for growth

<u>**Chapter 9: Facing Fear and Moving Forward**</u>

- Techniques for facing and overcoming fears
- Setting goals and taking action

<u>**Chapter 10: The Power of Positive Thinking**</u>

- The benefits of positive thinking
- How to cultivate a positive mindset

<u>**Chapter 11: Overcoming Fear and Taking Action**</u>

- Techniques for taking action despite fear
- Building momentum and staying motivated

<u>**Chapter 12: The Importance of Resilience in Overcoming Obstacles**</u>

- Further exploration of resilience and its role in overcoming challenges
- How to develop resilience in the face of adversity

<u>**Chapter 13: Building Resilience through Positive Self-Talk**</u>

- The impact of self-talk on resilience
- Techniques for cultivating positive self-talk

Chapter 14: Finding Motivation in the Face of Adversity

- Strategies for staying motivated during difficult times
- The importance of self-care and maintaining balance

Chapter 15: Finding Support Along the Way

- Additional strategies for building and maintaining a support system
- The benefits of seeking outside support

Chapter 16: Overcoming Fear and Doubt

- Advanced techniques for overcoming fear and doubt
- Practical exercises for building confidence

Chapter 17: Learning from Failure: Turning Setbacks into Opportunities for Growth

- Further exploration of failure and its role in personal growth
- Techniques for reframing failure as a learning opportunity

Chapter 18: The Power of Community: Finding Support and Strength in Others

- The benefits of community and collective strength
- Building and maintaining meaningful connections with others

Introduction:

Life is a journey full of twists and turns, and often, we encounter obstacles that seem insurmountable. These obstacles can make us question our destiny and leave us feeling stuck and unsure of what our future holds. However, it is important to remember that every obstacle we face is an opportunity for growth and learning. It is up to us to choose whether to let these obstacles hold us back or to use them as a stepping stone to our success.

In "Destined for Greatness: Overcoming Obstacles and Fulfilling Your Purpose," we will explore the various challenges that people face on their journey towards fulfilling their destiny. We will delve into the mindset and strategies necessary to overcome these obstacles and reach our full potential.

From recognizing our unique destiny to learning how to trust ourselves and our instincts, this book will guide us through 18 chapters of practical advice and inspiration to help us achieve our goals. Whether we are struggling with fear and self-doubt or navigating change and uncertainty, this book provides tools and techniques to overcome any obstacle and fulfill our purpose.

So, let us embark on this journey together, and discover what it truly means to be destined for greatness.
In this book, we will draw upon the experiences and wisdom of individuals who have overcome adversity and achieved success in their respective fields. Their stories will serve as inspiration and motivation for us to push through our own challenges and obstacles.

We will explore the power of positive thinking, the importance of perseverance, and the role of failure in achieving success. We will also discuss how to cultivate a growth mindset, overcome limiting beliefs, and find motivation even when we feel stuck.

Throughout this journey, we will also emphasize the importance of self-care and personal growth. We will learn how to celebrate our small wins and milestones and stay focused and disciplined in the pursuit of our dreams.

In the end, this book is a reminder that we are all destined for greatness, and it is up to us to overcome the obstacles that stand in our way. By embracing a positive mindset, learning from our failures, and staying focused on our purpose, we can achieve anything we set our minds to. So, let us begin this journey towards greatness, together.

Chapter 1:
Recognizing Your Unique Destiny

Do you ever feel like you were meant to do something great, but you just don't know what it is? Do you struggle to find your purpose and direction in life? You are not alone. Many people feel lost and unsure of their destiny, but the first step towards fulfilling your purpose is recognizing that you have a unique destiny.

Each one of us is born with certain talents, skills, and passions that make us unique. We all have a purpose in life, and it is up to us to discover what that purpose is. This can be a daunting task, but it is essential to recognize that we are all here for a reason.

One way to recognize your unique destiny is to reflect on your passions and interests. What activities bring you joy and fulfillment? What are you naturally good at? These are often clues to what your purpose may be. It is also helpful to consider what impact you want to make on the world. What issues or causes are you passionate about? How can you use your talents and skills to make a difference?

Another important factor to consider is your values and beliefs. What do you stand for? What do you want to be remembered for? These values and beliefs can guide you towards your purpose and help you stay true to your path.

Once you have a general idea of what your unique destiny may be, it is important to take action towards achieving it. This may involve taking risks, stepping out of your comfort zone, and facing challenges along the way. But remember, every obstacle is an opportunity for growth and learning.

So, take the time to reflect on your unique destiny. Recognize your talents, passions, and values, and take action towards achieving your purpose. You are destined for greatness, and the first step is recognizing your unique destiny.
It is important to note that recognizing your unique destiny is a journey, not a destination. You may find that your purpose evolves over time or that your passions change. It is okay to pivot and adapt as you grow and learn more about yourself.

Sometimes, it can be helpful to seek guidance from others when trying to recognize your unique destiny. This may involve talking to a mentor, a trusted friend or family member, or seeking professional guidance from a career counselor or life coach.

It is also important to recognize that our unique destiny is not always tied to a specific career or job title. Our purpose may manifest in different ways, such as volunteering, starting a business, or creating art.

In order to recognize our unique destiny, it is also important to let go of comparison and societal expectations. It can be tempting to compare ourselves to others or try to fit into societal norms, but this can often lead us away from our true purpose. We must embrace our individuality and trust that our unique path is the right one for us.

In conclusion, recognizing your unique destiny is the first step towards fulfilling your purpose and achieving greatness. By reflecting on your passions, values, and beliefs, and taking action towards your goals, you can uncover your unique destiny and make a meaningful impact on the world. Remember, the journey towards recognizing your unique destiny is a process, and it is okay to pivot and adapt as you grow and learn more about yourself.
Additionally, recognizing your unique destiny can help provide a sense of direction and focus in life. When we are aligned with our purpose, we feel more fulfilled, motivated, and energized. We are also more likely to overcome obstacles and setbacks because we know that we are working towards something meaningful.

However, recognizing your unique destiny is just the first step. It is important to take action towards your goals and dreams. This may involve setting specific, measurable, and achievable goals, and breaking them down into smaller, actionable steps. It may also involve seeking out resources, support, and guidance along the way.

It is also important to maintain a positive mindset and trust the process. Recognizing your unique destiny may involve taking risks and facing challenges, but it is important to approach these obstacles with a growth mindset. Failure is a natural part of the journey towards achieving greatness, and it is important to learn from our mistakes and keep moving forward.

Finally, recognizing your unique destiny can be a powerful tool for creating a life that is fulfilling and meaningful. By aligning with our purpose, we can make a positive impact on the world and leave a legacy that we can be proud of.

In conclusion, recognizing your unique destiny is a crucial step towards fulfilling your purpose and achieving greatness. By reflecting on your passions, values, and beliefs, and taking action towards your goals, you can uncover your unique destiny and create a life that is fulfilling and meaningful. Remember to maintain a positive mindset and trust the process, and don't be afraid to seek out support and guidance along the way. You are destined for greatness, and recognizing your unique destiny is just the beginning.

Chapter 2:
Overcoming Fear and Self-Doubt

As we strive to recognize and fulfill our unique destiny, we may encounter fear and self-doubt along the way. These negative emotions can hold us back from achieving our goals and living up to our potential. In order to overcome these obstacles, we must learn to recognize and address our fears and self-doubt.

Fear can take many forms, such as fear of failure, fear of rejection, or fear of the unknown. It is a natural human emotion, but it can become paralyzing if we allow it to control our actions. One way to overcome fear is to face it head-on. This may involve taking small steps towards your goal, gradually building up your confidence and resilience. It may also involve reframing your thoughts and beliefs about fear, recognizing that failure and setbacks are a natural part of the learning process.

Self-doubt is another obstacle that can hold us back from achieving our goals. It can take the form of negative self-talk, imposter syndrome, or feeling like we are not good enough. To overcome self-doubt, we must first recognize and acknowledge our negative thoughts and beliefs. We can then challenge these beliefs with evidence to the contrary, such as past successes or positive feedback from others. It is also important to surround ourselves with supportive people who believe in us and our potential.

In addition to facing our fears and self-doubt, it is important to cultivate a growth mindset. This involves embracing challenges and setbacks as opportunities for learning and growth, rather than seeing them as a reflection of our worth or abilities. We can also focus on our strengths and positive qualities, rather than dwelling on our weaknesses.

Another tool for overcoming fear and self-doubt is visualization. This involves visualizing yourself achieving your goals and living up to your potential. By imagining yourself succeeding, you can build up your confidence and motivation to take action towards your goals.

In conclusion, fear and self-doubt can be major obstacles on the journey towards recognizing and fulfilling our unique destiny. However, by facing our fears, challenging our negative beliefs, and cultivating a growth mindset, we can overcome these obstacles and achieve our goals. Remember to visualize yourself succeeding, focus on your strengths, and surround yourself with supportive people. You are capable of achieving greatness, and overcoming fear and self-doubt is the first step towards unlocking your potential.

It is also important to recognize that fear and self-doubt may never completely disappear. They may continue to surface as we encounter new challenges and opportunities in life. However, by building resilience and coping strategies, we can learn to manage these negative emotions and continue to move forward towards our goals.

One technique for managing fear and self-doubt is mindfulness. This involves being present and fully engaged in the present moment, rather than dwelling on past failures or worrying about future outcomes. By practicing mindfulness, we can reduce anxiety and increase our ability to focus on the task at hand.

Another technique is to reframe our thoughts and beliefs. Instead of seeing challenges as insurmountable obstacles, we can view them as opportunities for growth and development. This shift in perspective can help us to approach challenges with a more positive and proactive attitude.

It is also important to remember that failure is a natural part of the learning process. Every successful person has experienced setbacks and failures along the way. It is how we respond to these setbacks that ultimately determines our success. By reframing failure as an opportunity to learn and grow, we can develop resilience and increase our chances of success in the long run.

In conclusion, overcoming fear and self-doubt is a crucial step towards recognizing and fulfilling our unique destiny. By facing our fears, cultivating a growth mindset, and managing our negative thoughts and beliefs, we can overcome these obstacles and achieve our goals. Remember to practice mindfulness, reframe your thoughts, and embrace failure as an opportunity to learn and grow. You are capable of achieving greatness, and overcoming fear and self-doubt is the first step towards unlocking your potential.

It is important to recognize that fear and self-doubt can also be caused by external factors, such as societal expectations, pressure from family and friends, or even past traumatic experiences. In these cases, it may be helpful to seek support from a therapist or counselor, who can help us to work through these underlying issues and develop coping strategies.

Additionally, it can be helpful to set realistic goals and break them down into smaller, more manageable steps. This can help us to feel more in control of the situation and reduce feelings of overwhelm and anxiety. It is also important to celebrate our successes along the way, no matter how small they may be. This can help to build momentum and motivation as we continue towards our larger goals.

Another technique for overcoming fear and self-doubt is to practice self-compassion. This involves treating ourselves with kindness and understanding, rather than harsh criticism and self-judgment. By practicing self-compassion, we can reduce feelings of shame and self-doubt, and increase our resilience and ability to bounce back from setbacks.

In conclusion, overcoming fear and self-doubt is a complex process that involves addressing both internal and external factors. By seeking support, setting realistic goals, practicing self-compassion, and breaking down larger goals into smaller steps, we can gradually build up our confidence and resilience, and move towards fulfilling our unique destiny. Remember to be patient and kind to yourself along the way, and don't be afraid to seek support when you need it. You are capable of achieving greatness, and with perseverance and dedication, you can overcome fear and self-doubt and achieve your goals.

Chapter 3:
Developing Resilience

Resilience is the ability to bounce back from adversity, to adapt to change, and to cope with stress and challenges. Developing resilience is crucial for overcoming obstacles and fulfilling our destiny. In this chapter, we will explore some techniques for building resilience and developing the mental toughness necessary to achieve our goals.

One important aspect of resilience is maintaining a positive outlook. This involves focusing on our strengths and abilities, rather than dwelling on our weaknesses and limitations. It also involves cultivating a sense of gratitude for the good things in our lives, even in the face of adversity.

Another key aspect of resilience is cultivating a growth mindset. This involves viewing challenges as opportunities for growth and learning, rather than as insurmountable obstacles. It also involves embracing failure as a natural part of the learning process and recognizing that every setback is an opportunity to learn and improve.

Developing strong relationships and social support networks is also important for building resilience. Having a supportive network of family, friends, and mentors can provide us with the emotional support and encouragement we need to overcome challenges and pursue our goals.

Another important aspect of resilience is self-care. This involves taking care of our physical, emotional, and mental health through regular exercise, healthy eating, adequate sleep, and stress-reducing activities such as meditation and mindfulness.

In conclusion, developing resilience is crucial for overcoming obstacles and fulfilling our unique destiny. By maintaining a positive outlook, cultivating a growth mindset, building strong relationships and support networks, and practicing self-care, we can build the mental toughness necessary to achieve our goals. Remember to focus on your strengths, embrace failure as an opportunity to learn and grow, and take care of yourself along the way. With resilience and perseverance, you can overcome any obstacle and fulfill your destiny.

Moreover, developing resilience involves having the ability to manage stress and cope with adversity. One way to do this is by practicing mindfulness and staying present in the moment. This means focusing on the present, rather than worrying about the past or future. Mindfulness practices such as deep breathing, meditation, and yoga can help to reduce stress and promote relaxation.

In addition, developing resilience requires having a sense of purpose and meaning in life. This involves identifying our core values and beliefs, and aligning our actions and decisions with these values. Having a strong sense of purpose can provide us with the motivation and direction we need to overcome obstacles and achieve our goals.

Another technique for building resilience is practicing self-reflection. This involves taking the time to reflect on our experiences, emotions, and behaviors, and using this information to learn and grow. Self-reflection can help us to identify patterns in our thinking and behavior, and develop strategies for overcoming challenges and improving our lives.

Finally, it is important to recognize that building resilience is a lifelong process that requires ongoing effort and practice. It is not something that can be developed overnight or achieved without setbacks. However, by incorporating these techniques into our daily lives and remaining committed to our goals and values, we can gradually build the resilience and mental toughness necessary to overcome obstacles and fulfill our destiny.

In conclusion, developing resilience is a key component of overcoming obstacles and fulfilling our unique destiny. By maintaining a positive outlook, cultivating a growth mindset, building strong relationships and support networks, practicing self-care, managing stress, staying present, having a sense of purpose, and practicing self-reflection, we can build the mental toughness necessary to achieve our goals. Remember to stay committed to the process and believe in yourself, and you can overcome any obstacle and achieve your dreams.

In addition to the techniques mentioned above, another important aspect of developing resilience is having the ability to adapt to change. Life is full of unexpected twists and turns, and our ability to adapt to these changes can greatly impact our success in overcoming obstacles and fulfilling our destiny.

One way to develop adaptability is by being open to new experiences and ideas. This means stepping outside of our comfort zones and taking risks, even if it means facing the possibility of failure. By embracing new challenges and experiences, we can expand our knowledge and skills, and develop the flexibility necessary to adapt to change.

Another technique for developing adaptability is practicing problem-solving skills. This involves identifying problems or challenges, brainstorming possible solutions, and implementing the best solution. By practicing problem-solving skills, we can develop the ability to think creatively and find innovative solutions to difficult problems.

It is also important to remain flexible in our goals and plans. While it is important to have a clear direction and sense of purpose, it is also important to be open to adjusting our plans as needed in response to changing circumstances. This can involve being willing to change course, pivot, or take a different approach when necessary.

Finally, it is important to maintain a sense of optimism and hope, even in the face of adversity. This means focusing on the possibilities for growth and positive change, rather than dwelling on the negatives. By maintaining a positive outlook and believing in ourselves, we can cultivate the resilience and adaptability necessary to overcome any obstacle and fulfill our unique destiny.

In conclusion, developing resilience and adaptability are crucial components of overcoming obstacles and achieving our goals. By being open to new experiences and ideas, practicing problem-solving skills, remaining flexible in our goals and plans, and maintaining a sense of optimism and hope, we can develop the mental toughness necessary to navigate the challenges of life and fulfill our destiny. Remember to stay committed to your goals, stay flexible in your approach, and stay positive in your outlook, and you can overcome any obstacle and achieve your dreams.

Chapter 4:
Building a Support System

In life, we often face obstacles and challenges that we cannot overcome alone. That is why building a strong support system is an essential component of overcoming obstacles and fulfilling our destiny. A support system can provide us with the encouragement, guidance, and resources we need to navigate the challenges of life and achieve our goals.

One way to build a support system is by cultivating positive relationships with family and friends. This involves prioritizing our relationships, being there for others in their time of need, and seeking support when we need it. By building strong relationships with those closest to us, we can create a network of support that will be there for us through thick and thin.

Another way to build a support system is by seeking out mentors and role models. A mentor can provide us with guidance, advice, and support as we navigate the challenges of life and work towards our goals. By seeking out mentors who have achieved success in our desired field or area of interest, we can learn from their experiences and gain valuable insights that can help us to overcome obstacles and achieve our goals.

It is also important to seek out like-minded individuals who share our values and goals. This can involve joining groups or organizations that align with our interests and passions, or attending events or conferences where we can connect with others who share our aspirations. By surrounding ourselves with individuals who are supportive and encouraging, we can create a positive and uplifting environment that can help us to stay motivated and focused on our goals.

Finally, it is important to seek professional support when necessary. This can involve seeking the help of a therapist, coach, or other professional who can provide us with the guidance and support we need to overcome obstacles and achieve our goals. By seeking out professional support, we can gain valuable insights and strategies that can help us to navigate the challenges of life and fulfill our unique destiny.

In conclusion, building a support system is an essential component of overcoming obstacles and achieving our goals. By cultivating positive relationships with family and friends, seeking out mentors and role models, connecting with like-minded individuals, and seeking professional support when necessary, we can create a network of support that will be there for us through the ups and downs of life. Remember to prioritize your relationships, seek out guidance and support when needed, and surround yourself with individuals who uplift and encourage you, and you can overcome any obstacle and fulfill your destiny.

Moreover, building a support system can provide us with a sense of belonging and connection. This can help us to feel less isolated and alone when facing challenges, and can provide us with the emotional support we need to persevere. A strong support system can also provide us with practical resources, such as information, advice, and referrals to other professionals or resources.

However, building a support system requires effort and intentionality. It involves investing time and energy into our relationships and seeking out opportunities to connect with others who can support us in our goals. It may also involve being vulnerable and open with others, and asking for help when we need it.

In building a support system, it is important to also be mindful of the types of relationships we are cultivating. It is important to surround ourselves with individuals who are positive, encouraging, and supportive, and to distance ourselves from those who are negative or unsupportive. By being intentional about the relationships we cultivate, we can create a network of support that is conducive to our growth and success.

Additionally, it is important to recognize that our support system may evolve and change over time. As we grow and develop, our needs and goals may shift, and we may need to seek out new relationships and resources to support us in our new endeavors. It is important to remain open to new opportunities and to continue to invest in our relationships, even as they evolve and change.

In conclusion, building a support system is an essential component of overcoming obstacles and fulfilling our destiny. By investing in our relationships, seeking out guidance and support when needed, and being intentional about the types of relationships we cultivate, we can create a network of support that is conducive to our growth and success. Remember to stay open to new opportunities, invest in your relationships, and seek out guidance and support when needed, and you can overcome any obstacle and achieve your unique destiny.

Chapter 5:
Embracing Change and Adaptation

Life is full of changes and unexpected events that can disrupt our plans and goals. Whether it's a career change, a relationship breakdown, or a health issue, these challenges can be difficult to navigate and can leave us feeling lost and uncertain about the future. However, embracing change and adaptation is an essential component of overcoming obstacles and fulfilling our destiny.

One way to embrace change and adaptation is to cultivate a growth mindset. This involves viewing challenges and setbacks as opportunities for learning and growth, rather than as roadblocks to our success. By adopting a growth mindset, we can shift our focus from the negative aspects of a situation to the positive opportunities for growth and development.

Another way to embrace change and adaptation is to practice flexibility and adaptability. This involves being open to new experiences, ideas, and perspectives, and being willing to adjust our plans and goals as needed. By practicing flexibility and adaptability, we can learn to navigate change more effectively and can respond to unexpected events with greater resilience and resourcefulness.

It is also important to seek out opportunities for personal and professional development. This can involve attending workshops, taking courses, or seeking out mentorship or coaching. By investing in our own growth and development, we can increase our knowledge, skills, and abilities, and become better equipped to navigate change and adapt to new circumstances.

Finally, it is important to practice self-care and self-compassion during times of change and adaptation. This can involve taking care of our physical and emotional needs, such as getting enough sleep, eating well, and engaging in activities that bring us joy and fulfillment. It can also involve being gentle and kind to ourselves, and recognizing that change can be difficult and challenging, but that we have the strength and resilience to overcome it.

In conclusion, embracing change and adaptation is an essential component of overcoming obstacles and fulfilling our destiny. By cultivating a growth mindset, practicing flexibility and adaptability, seeking out opportunities for development, and practicing self-care and self-compassion, we can navigate change more effectively and respond to unexpected events with greater resilience and resourcefulness. Remember to stay open to new experiences and perspectives, invest in your own growth and development, and take care of yourself during times of change and adaptation, and you can overcome any obstacle and achieve your unique destiny.

Moreover, embracing change and adaptation requires us to be open to new possibilities and to let go of old ways of thinking and behaving that may no longer serve us. This can be challenging, as we may feel attached to our old ways of doing things and resistant to change. However, by letting go of our attachment to the past, we can create space for new growth and opportunities to emerge.

In addition, embracing change and adaptation involves being willing to take risks and step outside of our comfort zones. This can be scary, as it often involves facing uncertainty and the possibility of failure. However, by taking calculated risks and pushing ourselves to try new things, we can expand our horizons and discover new strengths and abilities.

It is important to recognize that change and adaptation are ongoing processes, and that we must continue to be open to new possibilities and opportunities as they arise. This means being willing to adapt our plans and goals as needed, and being open to feedback and guidance from others.

Finally, it is important to approach change and adaptation with a sense of curiosity and experimentation. Rather than viewing change as a negative or threatening event, we can approach it as an opportunity to learn and grow. By experimenting with new approaches and ideas, we can discover new ways of thinking and behaving that can help us to overcome obstacles and fulfill our destiny.

In conclusion, embracing change and adaptation is an essential component of overcoming obstacles and fulfilling our destiny. By being open to new possibilities, letting go of attachment to the past, taking risks and stepping outside of our comfort zones, and approaching change with a sense of curiosity and experimentation, we can navigate change and uncertainty more effectively and respond to unexpected events with greater resilience and resourcefulness. Remember to stay open to new opportunities and to be willing to adapt and experiment as needed, and you can overcome any obstacle and achieve your unique destiny.

Furthermore, embracing change and adaptation requires us to develop a strong sense of self-awareness. This involves being aware of our thoughts, emotions, and behaviors, and how they may be influencing our responses to change and uncertainty. By developing self-awareness, we can become more conscious of our habits and patterns, and can identify areas where we may need to make changes in order to adapt more effectively.

Another key component of embracing change and adaptation is cultivating a sense of resilience. This involves developing the ability to bounce back from setbacks and failures, and to remain optimistic and hopeful in the face of adversity. By building resilience, we can approach change and uncertainty with a sense of confidence and resourcefulness, knowing that we have the skills and abilities to overcome any obstacle.

It is also important to seek out support and connection during times of change and adaptation. This can involve reaching out to friends, family, or professional networks for advice and guidance, or joining support groups or communities that share our interests and goals. By connecting with others who share our experiences and challenges, we can find encouragement and inspiration, and can learn from their experiences and insights.

Finally, embracing change and adaptation requires us to maintain a sense of purpose and meaning in our lives. This means staying connected to our values, passions, and goals, even in the face of uncertainty and change. By staying true to our purpose and vision, we can remain motivated and focused, and can overcome any obstacle that stands in the way of our destiny.

In conclusion, embracing change and adaptation is an essential component of overcoming obstacles and fulfilling our destiny. By developing self-awareness, cultivating resilience, seeking out support and connection, and maintaining a sense of purpose and meaning, we can navigate change and uncertainty with greater ease and grace. Remember to stay connected to your values and goals, and to seek out support and connection during times of change and adaptation, and

you can overcome any obstacle and achieve your
unique destiny.

Chapter 6:
Overcoming Fear and Doubt

Fear and doubt are two of the most common obstacles that we face on the path to fulfilling our destiny. Whether it is fear of failure, fear of rejection, or doubt about our abilities and worthiness, these emotions can hold us back and prevent us from taking the risks necessary to achieve our goals.

The first step in overcoming fear and doubt is to acknowledge and accept these emotions as a normal part of the human experience. It is natural to feel afraid or uncertain when we are stepping outside of our comfort zones or facing new challenges. However, it is important not to let these emotions paralyze us or prevent us from taking action.

One way to overcome fear and doubt is to focus on our strengths and past successes. By reflecting on times when we have overcome obstacles or achieved our goals, we can build confidence in our abilities and trust in our capacity to succeed. It is also helpful to set small, achievable goals that build upon our strengths and allow us to make progress towards our larger goals.

Another strategy for overcoming fear and doubt is to reframe our negative self-talk and limiting beliefs. Instead of focusing on what could go wrong or on our perceived weaknesses, we can focus on what we have to gain and on the possibilities that exist when we take action. By shifting our mindset from one of fear and doubt to one of possibility and opportunity, we can cultivate a more positive and empowered outlook on our lives and our goals.

It is also important to practice self-care and to cultivate a support network of friends, family, and mentors who can provide encouragement and guidance during times of doubt and fear. This can involve engaging in activities that bring us joy and relaxation, such as exercise, meditation, or creative pursuits. It can also involve seeking out the advice and support of others who have faced similar challenges and who can offer insight and perspective on our situation.

In conclusion, fear and doubt are common obstacles that we face on the path to fulfilling our destiny. However, by acknowledging and accepting these emotions, focusing on our strengths and past successes, reframing negative self-talk and limiting beliefs, practicing self-care, and seeking out support and guidance, we can overcome these obstacles and achieve our goals with greater confidence and resilience. Remember to stay focused on your strengths and to seek out support when needed, and you can overcome any obstacle and achieve your unique destiny.

Another helpful approach to overcoming fear and doubt is to confront and challenge our limiting beliefs directly. Often, our fears and doubts stem from deeply ingrained beliefs about ourselves and our abilities that may not be accurate or helpful. By examining these beliefs and questioning their validity, we can begin to break free from their hold on us and create new, more empowering beliefs.

This process of challenging and reframing limiting beliefs can be done through various techniques, such as journaling, therapy, or coaching. It involves identifying the thoughts and beliefs that are holding us back, examining the evidence for and against these beliefs, and replacing them with more accurate and positive beliefs that support our goals and aspirations.

Another important aspect of overcoming fear and doubt is to cultivate a growth mindset. This means embracing the idea that our abilities and potential are not fixed, but can be developed and improved with effort and practice. By focusing on learning and growth rather than on the outcome or the fear of failure, we can approach challenges with a more positive and resilient attitude, and view obstacles as opportunities for growth and development.

Finally, it is important to remember that overcoming fear and doubt is not a one-time event, but an ongoing process. As we continue to pursue our goals and face new challenges, we may encounter new fears and doubts that need to be addressed. By cultivating a mindset of self-awareness, self-compassion, and continuous learning and growth, we can navigate these obstacles with greater ease and confidence, and move closer towards fulfilling our unique destiny.

Chapter 7:
Building Resilience

Resilience is the ability to bounce back from setbacks and overcome adversity. It is an essential quality for anyone seeking to fulfill their destiny, as obstacles and challenges are inevitable on the path to success.

Building resilience involves developing a set of skills and practices that help us cope with stress, adapt to change, and maintain a positive outlook in the face of adversity. These skills can be cultivated through various means, such as mindfulness, exercise, social support, and cognitive-behavioral therapy.

One effective way to build resilience is through mindfulness meditation. Mindfulness involves paying attention to the present moment without judgment, and can help us develop a greater sense of awareness and control over our thoughts and emotions. By practicing mindfulness regularly, we can become more resilient to stress and better able to cope with difficult situations.

Exercise is another powerful tool for building resilience. Physical activity has been shown to reduce symptoms of anxiety and depression, improve mood, and increase self-esteem. By incorporating regular exercise into our daily routines, we can strengthen our bodies and minds, and better equip ourselves to face the challenges of life.

Social support is also crucial for building resilience. Having a network of supportive friends, family, and mentors can provide us with the encouragement, guidance, and perspective that we need to overcome adversity. It is important to cultivate these relationships and to reach out for help when we need it, rather than trying to tackle challenges alone.

Cognitive-behavioral therapy (CBT) is a type of therapy that focuses on identifying and changing negative thought patterns and behaviors. By working with a therapist trained in CBT, we can learn to reframe our thoughts and beliefs in more positive and empowering ways, and develop strategies for coping with stress and adversity.

In conclusion, building resilience is an essential part of fulfilling our destiny. By developing mindfulness and meditation practices, incorporating regular exercise into our routines, cultivating social support, and seeking out therapy when needed, we can strengthen our ability to cope with setbacks and challenges, and maintain a positive and resilient outlook on life. Remember that resilience is a skill that can be developed with practice and persistence, and that by building this quality, we can overcome any obstacle and achieve our unique destiny.

Another effective way to build resilience is by developing a growth mindset. This means viewing challenges and setbacks as opportunities for learning and growth, rather than as evidence of our limitations or failures. By embracing a growth mindset, we can approach difficulties with a more positive and flexible attitude, and use them as opportunities to develop new skills and knowledge.

It is also important to practice self-care as a way of building resilience. This involves taking care of our physical, emotional, and mental well-being through activities such as getting enough sleep, eating a healthy diet, engaging in hobbies and activities that bring us joy, and seeking out professional help when needed.

Finally, it is important to cultivate a sense of purpose and meaning in our lives as a way of building resilience. This can involve setting meaningful goals, engaging in activities that align with our values and passions, and seeking out ways to contribute to something larger than ourselves. By having a strong sense of purpose and direction in life, we can find the motivation and resilience needed to overcome obstacles and fulfill our destiny.

In summary, building resilience is a crucial component of overcoming obstacles and fulfilling our unique destiny. By developing mindfulness and meditation practices, incorporating regular exercise into our routines, cultivating social support, embracing a growth mindset, practicing self-care, and cultivating a sense of purpose and meaning in our lives, we can strengthen our ability to bounce back from setbacks and navigate the challenges of life with greater ease and confidence.

Chapter 8:
Embracing Failure as a Stepping Stone

Failure is an inevitable part of life, and especially on the path towards fulfilling our destiny. However, many people view failure as a setback, a sign of weakness or incompetence, or even as a reason to give up. In reality, failure can be a powerful tool for growth and development, and a stepping stone towards success.

One way to embrace failure as a stepping stone is to reframe our mindset around it. Rather than viewing failure as a negative experience, we can see it as an opportunity for learning and growth. Failure can help us identify areas where we need to improve, adjust our approach to challenges, and develop new skills and knowledge.

Another way to embrace failure as a stepping stone is to practice self-compassion. Self-compassion involves treating ourselves with kindness and understanding, rather than with self-criticism or judgment. By practicing self-compassion, we can acknowledge our mistakes and shortcomings without getting bogged down by shame or self-doubt, and instead use these experiences as opportunities for growth and development.

It is also important to cultivate resilience in the face of failure. Building resilience involves developing a set of skills and practices that help us cope with stress and adversity, such as mindfulness, exercise, social support, and cognitive-behavioral therapy. By building resilience, we can approach failure with greater ease and confidence, and use it as a stepping stone towards success.

Finally, it is important to remember that failure is not an end point, but rather a part of the journey towards fulfilling our destiny. By persevering through failure, learning from our mistakes, and continuing to move forward towards our goals, we can achieve the success we desire.

In conclusion, embracing failure as a stepping stone is an essential component of fulfilling our unique destiny. By reframing our mindset around failure, practicing self-compassion, cultivating resilience, and persevering through setbacks, we can use failure as an opportunity for growth and development, and ultimately achieve the success we desire.

Another important aspect of embracing failure as a stepping stone is to shift our focus from the outcome to the process. When we focus solely on achieving a specific outcome, we may become overly fixated on success and fear failure. However, when we shift our focus to the process of growth and development, we can view failure as a natural part of the journey towards achieving our goals.

This means breaking down our goals into smaller, more manageable steps, and celebrating the progress we make along the way. By embracing the process, we can recognize that failure is not a reflection of our worth or abilities, but rather a normal part of the learning process.

It is also important to reframe how we view failure in relation to our identity. Many people tie their self-worth to their achievements or failures, leading to a fear of failure and a negative self-image. However, by separating our sense of self from our achievements, we can view failure as a temporary setback rather than a reflection of our identity.

Additionally, seeking out support from others can be helpful in embracing failure as a stepping stone. This can involve seeking out feedback and advice from mentors or peers, or simply sharing our experiences with others who can offer encouragement and support.

In summary, embracing failure as a stepping stone involves shifting our mindset from viewing failure as a negative experience to seeing it as an opportunity for growth and development. This includes focusing on the process of growth and development, separating our sense of self from our achievements, seeking out support from others, and cultivating resilience in the face of setbacks. By embracing failure as a natural part of the journey towards fulfilling our destiny, we can achieve greater success and fulfillment in our lives.

Chapter 9:
Facing Fear and Moving Forward

Fear is a natural and necessary emotion that helps us to stay safe and avoid danger. However, when fear becomes overwhelming, it can hold us back from pursuing our goals and fulfilling our destiny. In this chapter, we will explore how to face our fears and move forward with courage and confidence.

The first step in facing our fears is to identify and acknowledge them. This means taking the time to reflect on what is holding us back and why we are afraid. Once we have identified our fears, we can begin to examine them more closely and challenge the assumptions and beliefs that underlie them.

One effective strategy for facing fear is to gradually expose ourselves to the things that scare us. This can involve setting small, achievable goals that gradually build up our confidence and help us to overcome our fears. For example, if we are afraid of public speaking, we could start by speaking in front of a small group of friends or colleagues, and gradually work our way up to larger audiences.

Another important aspect of facing fear is developing a mindset of resilience and perseverance. This means recognizing that setbacks and failures are a natural part of the journey towards achieving our goals, and that we can learn from them and grow stronger as a result.

It is also important to surround ourselves with supportive people who can offer encouragement and guidance as we face our fears. This may involve seeking out mentors, joining support groups, or simply spending time with friends and family who believe in us and our abilities.

Ultimately, facing our fears requires courage, perseverance, and a willingness to take risks. By acknowledging and challenging our fears, taking small steps towards our goals, and cultivating a supportive mindset, we can overcome our fears and move forward with confidence towards our destiny.

In the next chapter, we will explore the importance of cultivating a positive mindset and overcoming negative self-talk.

Additionally, reframing our mindset around failure can help us to face our fears. Instead of seeing failure as a negative outcome, we can view it as a natural part of the learning process and an opportunity for growth. This can help to reduce the fear of failure and give us the confidence to take risks and pursue our goals.

Another effective strategy for facing fear is to focus on the present moment and taking things one step at a time. Often, our fears are related to future outcomes or worst-case scenarios that may never come to pass. By staying grounded in the present moment and focusing on the task at hand, we can reduce our anxiety and build our confidence.

Lastly, it is important to remember that facing our fears is a process that takes time and effort. It is normal to experience setbacks and challenges along the way, and we may not always succeed on the first try. However, by staying committed to our goals and persevering in the face of fear, we can overcome our limitations and achieve our true potential.

In summary, facing our fears is a crucial step in fulfilling our destiny. By identifying and acknowledging our fears, gradually exposing ourselves to the things that scare us, developing a resilient mindset, cultivating a support network, reframing our mindset around failure, focusing on the present moment, and persevering through setbacks and challenges, we can overcome our fears and move forward towards our goals.

Chapter 10:
The Power of Positive Thinking

Our thoughts have a powerful influence on our emotions, actions, and outcomes. If we constantly think negative thoughts and expect the worst, we are likely to feel discouraged, unmotivated, and unfulfilled. On the other hand, if we cultivate a positive mindset and focus on our strengths and opportunities, we are more likely to feel confident, motivated, and successful. In this chapter, we will explore the importance of positive thinking in overcoming obstacles and achieving our destiny.

Positive thinking involves focusing on our strengths and potential, rather than our weaknesses and limitations. It means looking for the silver lining in difficult situations, finding opportunities for growth and learning, and believing in ourselves and our abilities. This doesn't mean ignoring or denying the challenges and obstacles we face, but rather approaching them with a solution-focused and optimistic mindset.

One effective way to cultivate positive thinking is through affirmations. Affirmations are positive statements that we repeat to ourselves to reinforce positive beliefs and attitudes. For example, we might say to ourselves, "I am capable of overcoming any obstacle," or "I am worthy of success and happiness." By repeating these affirmations regularly, we can train our minds to focus on the positive and develop a more optimistic outlook.

Another important aspect of positive thinking is visualization. Visualization involves imagining ourselves achieving our goals and experiencing positive outcomes. By visualizing our success and focusing on the positive emotions associated with it, we can increase our motivation and confidence, and create a sense of momentum towards our goals.

It is also important to surround ourselves with positive influences, such as supportive friends and mentors, uplifting books and media, and positive role models. By surrounding ourselves with positivity, we can create a more optimistic and empowering environment for ourselves.

In summary, positive thinking is a powerful tool for overcoming obstacles and achieving our destiny. By focusing on our strengths and potential, using affirmations and visualization, and surrounding ourselves with positivity, we can cultivate a more optimistic and empowering mindset that helps us to overcome challenges and achieve our goals. In the next chapter, we will explore the importance of resilience in the face of adversity.

Another important aspect of positive thinking is gratitude. Gratitude involves focusing on the positive aspects of our lives and being thankful for them. It can help us to develop a more positive outlook, reduce stress, and improve our overall well-being. By focusing on what we have rather than what we lack, we can cultivate a sense of abundance and positivity in our lives.

In addition to cultivating positive thinking, it's important to take action towards our goals. Positive thinking alone won't lead to success unless we also take concrete steps towards achieving our goals. This means setting clear goals, developing a plan of action, and taking consistent steps towards our goals. By taking action, we can build momentum towards our goals and increase our sense of confidence and control.

It's also important to be open to learning and growth. When we encounter obstacles or setbacks, it's easy to become discouraged and give up. However, by approaching these challenges with a growth mindset, we can view them as opportunities for learning and growth. By reflecting on what we can learn from our experiences and making adjustments as needed, we can overcome obstacles and continue to progress towards our goals.

Finally, it's important to recognize that positive thinking is not a magic solution to all of our problems. We will inevitably encounter setbacks and challenges along the way, and it's important to be prepared for these obstacles. This means developing resilience and perseverance, and being willing to adapt and make changes as needed.

In conclusion, positive thinking is a powerful tool for overcoming obstacles and achieving our destiny. By cultivating a positive mindset, focusing on our strengths and potential, and taking action towards our goals, we can increase our sense of confidence, motivation, and success. By also being open to learning and growth, and recognizing that setbacks and challenges are a natural part of the journey, we can develop resilience and persevere through obstacles towards our desired destiny.

Chapter 11:
Overcoming fear and Take Action

In life, we are faced with various fears that can hold us back from achieving our goals and dreams. Fear can come in different forms such as fear of failure, fear of rejection, fear of the unknown, and many others. However, it is essential to understand that fear is a natural emotion that can be overcome. In this chapter, we will discuss how to overcome fear and take action towards achieving our goals.Identify your fears:
The first step towards overcoming fear is to identify what you are afraid of. Take time to reflect on your thoughts and emotions to understand what is holding you back. Once you have identified your fears, write them down and confront them.

Understand the root cause:
It is essential to understand the root cause of your fears. Sometimes, our fears may stem from past experiences or trauma. Understanding the root cause will help you to deal with the fears more effectively.

Once you have identified and understood your fears, it is time to challenge them. Ask yourself questions such as, "what is the worst that can happen?" or "what can I do to prepare for the worst-case scenario?" Challenging your fears will help you to see that they are not as big and scary as they seem.

<u>Take action:</u>

The next step is to take action towards overcoming your fears. Start with small steps that can help build your confidence. For instance, if you are afraid of public speaking, start by speaking in front of a small group of people and gradually build your way up.

<u>Visualize success:</u>

Visualization is a powerful tool that can help you overcome your fears. Visualize yourself succeeding in whatever it is you are afraid of. This will help to build your confidence and make you more comfortable with taking risks.

<u>Get support:</u>

Finally, it is essential to have a support system that can help you overcome your fears. Surround yourself with people who encourage and motivate you to take action towards achieving your goals.

Another important step is to challenge our negative thoughts and beliefs. Often, fear and self-doubt are fueled by negative self-talk and limiting beliefs. For example, we may tell ourselves that we're not good enough, or that we'll never succeed. By challenging these negative thoughts and replacing them with positive, empowering beliefs, we can begin to shift our mindset and gain more confidence in ourselves.

It's also important to take action despite our fear and self-doubt. This means taking risks and stepping outside of our comfort zones, even when we feel scared or uncertain. By taking action, we can prove to ourselves that we are capable and competent, which can help to boost our confidence and reduce our self-doubt.

Another helpful strategy is to surround ourselves with positive, supportive people who believe in us and our abilities. When we have a strong support system, we are more likely to feel confident and motivated to pursue our goals.

Finally, it's important to remember that fear and self-doubt are natural emotions that everyone experiences at some point. We don't have to let these emotions hold us back from achieving our destiny. By acknowledging our fear and self-doubt, and taking steps to overcome them, we can move towards our goals with confidence and courage.

In conclusion, overcoming fear and self-doubt is essential for achieving our destiny. By identifying the source of these negative emotions, challenging our negative thoughts and beliefs, taking action despite our fears, surrounding ourselves with positive support, and acknowledging that fear and self-doubt are natural emotions, we can gain the confidence and courage we need to succeed.

In addition to the strategies mentioned above, there are a few more techniques that can help us overcome fear and self-doubt.

Visualization is a powerful tool that can help us overcome our fears and doubts. By visualizing ourselves succeeding, we can create a positive mindset and reduce our anxiety about the future. For example, if we're nervous about giving a presentation, we can visualize ourselves giving the presentation confidently and effectively.

Another technique is to practice self-compassion. Often, we are our own worst critics and can be very hard on ourselves when we make mistakes or encounter challenges. By practicing self-compassion, we can learn to treat ourselves with kindness and understanding, which can help us feel more confident and resilient.

It's also important to celebrate our successes, no matter how small they may be. By acknowledging and celebrating our achievements, we can boost our self-esteem and feel more confident in our abilities.

Finally, it can be helpful to remind ourselves of our purpose and why we are pursuing our destiny. By focusing on our larger goals and the impact we want to make in the world, we can find the motivation and courage we need to overcome our fears and doubts.
Conclusion:

Fear is a natural emotion that can hold us back from achieving our dreams. However, with the right mindset and approach, we can overcome our fears and take action towards our goals. Remember to identify your fears, understand the root cause, challenge your fears, take action, visualize success, and get support.

Chapter 12:
The Importance of Resilience in Overcoming Obstacles

Inevitably, as we pursue our destiny, we will encounter obstacles and setbacks along the way. These obstacles may take many forms, such as rejection, failure, criticism, or unexpected challenges. However, the key to overcoming these obstacles is resilience.

Resilience is the ability to bounce back from adversity and to persevere in the face of challenges. It involves developing a mindset that allows us to view setbacks as opportunities for growth and learning, rather than as evidence of our inadequacy or failure.

One of the ways to cultivate resilience is through the practice of gratitude. By focusing on the things we are grateful for, even in the midst of adversity, we can develop a more positive outlook and increase our resilience. This can help us to keep going when things get tough, and to find meaning and purpose in our struggles.

Another way to build resilience is to develop a support system. This may involve seeking out mentors, friends, or family members who can provide encouragement, guidance, and a listening ear when we need it. It may also involve connecting with others who are on a similar path, and sharing our experiences and challenges with them.

Finally, it's important to remember that resilience is not something that we either have or don't have. Rather, it is a skill that can be developed and strengthened over time. By practicing gratitude, building a support system, and developing a growth mindset, we can cultivate resilience and overcome the obstacles that stand in the way of our destiny.

In conclusion, resilience is a crucial component of overcoming obstacles and achieving our destiny. By developing a mindset of growth, practicing gratitude, building a support system, and cultivating resilience, we can persevere in the face of adversity and move closer to realizing our dreams.

Resilience is not only important for overcoming obstacles in our personal lives but also in our professional lives. In the workplace, we may face challenges such as layoffs, difficult coworkers or bosses, or unexpected changes in our job responsibilities. Developing resilience can help us to adapt to these changes and to continue to perform at a high level.

One way to build resilience in the workplace is to focus on developing a growth mindset. This means embracing challenges and seeing them as opportunities for growth and development. By viewing setbacks as opportunities to learn and improve, we can develop a more positive outlook on our work and increase our resilience.

Another important aspect of resilience in the workplace is developing strong relationships with coworkers and supervisors. This can involve seeking out mentors or allies who can provide guidance and support, as well as developing strong communication and conflict resolution skills.

Finally, it's important to take care of our physical and emotional well-being in order to build resilience. This may involve practicing self-care techniques such as meditation, exercise, or journaling, as well as seeking out professional support if needed.

In sum, developing resilience is crucial for overcoming obstacles and achieving our destiny in both our personal and professional lives. By cultivating a growth mindset, building strong relationships, and taking care of our physical and emotional well-being, we can develop the resilience needed to thrive in the face of adversity.

Chapter 13
Building resilience through positive self-talk.

One of the most significant obstacles we may face in life is fear. Fear can hold us back from taking risks, pursuing our dreams, and reaching our full potential. In chapter 13, we will explore strategies for overcoming fear and building the confidence we need to achieve our destiny.

One way to overcome fear is to break it down into smaller, manageable steps. By taking small steps toward our goals, we can gradually build our confidence and momentum. This may involve setting small goals and celebrating our progress along the way.

Another strategy for overcoming fear is to practice self-compassion. This means being kind to ourselves and acknowledging that it's okay to make mistakes or experience setbacks along the way. By treating ourselves with compassion, we can reduce the fear of failure and build our resilience.

It's also important to challenge our limiting beliefs and negative self-talk. We may have internalized beliefs about ourselves or our abilities that hold us back from reaching our potential. By questioning these beliefs and replacing them with more positive, empowering thoughts, we can build our confidence and overcome our fears.

Finally, seeking support from others can be a powerful tool for overcoming fear. This may involve working with a therapist or coach, or simply seeking out the encouragement and guidance of friends and family members.

By utilizing these strategies, we can overcome fear and build the confidence we need to pursue our dreams and achieve our destiny.

Additionally, facing our fears head-on can also be an effective way to overcome them. This may involve taking risks and stepping outside of our comfort zone, even if it feels scary at first. By pushing ourselves to face our fears, we can build our confidence and resilience in the face of adversity.

Visualization and positive affirmations can also be helpful in overcoming fear. By visualizing ourselves succeeding and achieving our goals, we can build a positive and empowering mindset. Additionally, repeating positive affirmations to ourselves can help to shift our thoughts from fear and self-doubt to confidence and self-assurance.

Ultimately, overcoming fear is a process that requires patience, persistence, and self-compassion. By breaking down our fears into manageable steps, practicing self-compassion, challenging limiting beliefs, seeking support, facing our fears, and utilizing visualization and positive affirmations, we can build the confidence and resilience needed to achieve our destiny.

Chapter 14:
Finding motivation in the face of adversity.

In chapter 14, we will explore the importance of resilience in overcoming obstacles and achieving our destiny. Resilience refers to the ability to adapt and bounce back from difficult situations or setbacks.

Resilience is not something we are born with, but rather a skill that can be developed and strengthened over time. One key aspect of resilience is having a growth mindset, which means seeing challenges and setbacks as opportunities for growth and learning.

Another important aspect of resilience is building a support system. Having a network of supportive friends, family, and mentors can help us navigate difficult situations and provide us with the encouragement and guidance we need to keep going.

Practicing self-care is also crucial for building resilience. This may involve getting enough sleep, eating a healthy diet, exercising regularly, and taking time for activities that bring us joy and relaxation.

Developing problem-solving and coping skills is also important for building resilience. This may involve learning new skills, seeking out resources, and developing healthy ways to cope with stress and difficult emotions.

Ultimately, building resilience takes time and effort, but it is a key ingredient in achieving our destiny. By cultivating a growth mindset, building a support system, practicing self-care, and developing problem-solving and coping skills, we can become more resilient and better equipped to overcome obstacles and achieve our goals.

Another important aspect of resilience is developing a sense of purpose and meaning in our lives. When we have a clear sense of our values and goals, we are better able to navigate challenges and setbacks, as we have a sense of what we are working towards.

Having a sense of purpose can also provide us with motivation and inspiration, helping us to persevere through difficult times. This may involve identifying our passions and interests, and finding ways to incorporate them into our work and personal lives.

Another key aspect of resilience is learning to manage our emotions effectively. This involves developing emotional regulation skills, such as mindfulness and relaxation techniques, that can help us stay calm and centered in the face of adversity.

Finally, it is important to recognize that setbacks and failures are a natural part of the journey towards achieving our destiny. Rather than giving up in the face of failure, it is important to view setbacks as opportunities for growth and learning, and to use them as motivation to keep going.

By developing resilience, we can become more adept at navigating the challenges and obstacles that inevitably arise on the path towards achieving our destiny. Whether it is developing a growth mindset, building a support system, practicing self-care, developing problem-solving and coping skills, finding purpose and meaning, managing our emotions effectively, or learning from setbacks and failures, there are many tools and strategies we can use to cultivate resilience and become more resilient in the face of adversity.

Chapter 15
Finding Support Along the Way

One of the most important factors in overcoming obstacles and achieving our destiny is having a strong support system. This may include friends, family members, mentors, coaches, or colleagues who can offer guidance, encouragement, and practical support as we pursue our goals.

Having a support system can provide us with a sense of belonging and connection, which can be essential for maintaining our motivation and resilience in the face of adversity. It can also offer us new perspectives and ideas, and help us identify opportunities we may not have seen otherwise.

In order to build a strong support system, it is important to be intentional about seeking out and nurturing relationships with people who share our values and goals. This may involve joining groups or organizations related to our interests, seeking out mentors or coaches in our field, or simply being open to meeting new people and building meaningful connections.

It is also important to be willing to ask for help when we need it, and to be willing to offer help and support to others in our network. By building strong relationships with others who are also committed to achieving their goals, we can create a community of support that can help us overcome obstacles and achieve success.

In this chapter, we will explore the importance of building a support system, and offer strategies for identifying and nurturing meaningful relationships with people who can help us achieve our destiny. Whether it is through joining professional organizations, seeking out mentors and coaches, or simply being open to building new connections, there are many ways to build a strong support system that can help us navigate the challenges and obstacles that inevitably arise on the path to success.

When it comes to finding support along the way, it is important to seek out individuals who not only share our goals, but also have the skills, experience, and knowledge that can help us grow and succeed. For example, if we are pursuing a career in a specific field, it may be helpful to seek out mentors or coaches who have experience and connections in that field. These individuals can offer guidance and advice, and can help us navigate the challenges and opportunities that arise in our chosen profession.

Another important aspect of building a strong support system is being willing to give and receive feedback. Constructive feedback can help us identify areas where we need to improve, and can help us grow and develop as individuals. It is important to be open to feedback, and to view it as an opportunity for growth rather than as a criticism.

In addition to seeking out individual mentors and coaches, it can also be helpful to join groups or organizations related to our interests or goals. These groups can offer us a sense of community, and can provide opportunities to connect with others who share our passions and ambitions. They can also offer valuable resources and networking opportunities, which can be essential for achieving our goals.

Finally, it is important to remember that building a strong support system takes time and effort. It requires us to be intentional about the relationships we build, and to be willing to invest time and energy into nurturing those relationships over the long-term. By doing so, we can create a network of individuals who are committed to our success, and who can provide us with the guidance, encouragement, and support we need to overcome obstacles and achieve our destiny.

In summary, finding support along the way is essential for achieving our goals and overcoming obstacles on the path to success. By seeking out mentors, coaches, and community organizations, and by being open to giving and receiving feedback, we can build a strong support system that can help us navigate the challenges and opportunities of our chosen path. Ultimately, it is through the support and encouragement of others that we can achieve our greatest potential and fulfill our destiny.

Chapter 16
Overcoming Fear and Doubt

Fear and doubt are natural emotions that can arise when we are faced with uncertainty or challenges. However, when left unchecked, they can become powerful barriers to our success and prevent us from achieving our destiny.

One of the keys to overcoming fear and doubt is to recognize them for what they are: normal human emotions that can be managed and overcome. Instead of allowing ourselves to be consumed by these emotions, we can learn to acknowledge them, examine them, and take steps to move past them.

One technique for managing fear and doubt is to practice mindfulness. By becoming more aware of our thoughts and emotions, we can begin to identify when fear and doubt are taking hold, and can take steps to counteract them. This might involve practicing relaxation techniques, such as deep breathing or meditation, or engaging in activities that bring us joy and help us to stay grounded.

Another important step in overcoming fear and doubt is to challenge our negative self-talk. Often, our fears and doubts are fueled by negative beliefs and assumptions about ourselves and our abilities. By questioning these beliefs and examining the evidence, we can begin to see them for what they are: unfounded and limiting. Instead, we can focus on our strengths and accomplishments, and remind ourselves that we are capable of achieving great things.

It is also important to seek out support and encouragement from others. Talking to a trusted friend, mentor, or coach can help us to gain perspective and develop strategies for overcoming our fears and doubts. They can also provide us with the motivation and accountability we need to stay focused on our goals and overcome obstacles along the way.

Ultimately, the key to overcoming fear and doubt is to take action. By setting goals and taking small, incremental steps towards achieving them, we can build momentum and confidence, and begin to see that we are capable of overcoming any obstacle that comes our way. By persisting in the face of fear and doubt, and by continuing to learn and grow, we can achieve our destiny and live a life that is fulfilling and meaningful.

Overcoming fear and doubt is not a one-time event but a continuous process. We must learn to recognize when these emotions arise and develop strategies to overcome them. It is a journey that requires patience, perseverance, and self-compassion.

One effective strategy for managing fear and doubt is to practice positive self-talk. We can reframe negative thoughts and beliefs into positive affirmations that reinforce our confidence and abilities. For example, instead of thinking "I can't do this," we can say "I am capable and competent."

Another useful technique is to visualize success. By visualizing ourselves achieving our goals and experiencing the feelings of accomplishment and satisfaction that come with it, we can train our minds to focus on positive outcomes and build our confidence in our ability to succeed.

In addition, it is important to remember that failure is a natural part of the learning process. Instead of allowing failure to feed our fears and doubts, we can reframe it as an opportunity for growth and learning. By embracing a growth mindset and viewing challenges as opportunities for growth and improvement, we can develop resilience and overcome obstacles more effectively.

In conclusion, overcoming fear and doubt is essential for achieving our destiny. By recognizing these emotions as natural and manageable, and by developing strategies to overcome them, we can build our confidence and take action towards our goals. With perseverance and a growth mindset, we can overcome any obstacle and achieve our true potential.

Chapter 17
Learning from failure: turning setbacks into opportunities for growth.

One of the biggest obstacles to achieving our destiny is the fear of failure. Many of us have a deep-seated fear of failing and making mistakes, which can hold us back from taking risks and pursuing our dreams.

However, it is important to understand that failure is not the end of the road. In fact, many successful people have experienced multiple failures before achieving their ultimate success. It is through failure that we can learn and grow, and ultimately become better equipped to handle future challenges.

One key to overcoming the fear of failure is to reframe our perspective on it. Instead of viewing failure as a negative outcome, we can view it as a necessary step towards success. We can also focus on the lessons learned from each failure, and use those lessons to make better decisions in the future.

Another strategy is to develop a growth mindset. This means embracing challenges as opportunities for growth and viewing setbacks as temporary obstacles that can be overcome with effort and persistence. By adopting a growth mindset, we can build resilience and develop the confidence to take risks and pursue our goals.

Finally, it is important to surround ourselves with a supportive community. Having people who believe in us and our abilities can provide the encouragement and motivation we need to keep pushing forward, even in the face of failure.

In conclusion, the fear of failure is a common obstacle on the journey towards our destiny. However, by reframing our perspective, developing a growth mindset, and surrounding ourselves with support, we can overcome this fear and move closer towards our goals.

Another obstacle that can impede our progress towards our destiny is self-doubt. This is the inner voice that tells us we are not good enough, smart enough, or capable enough to achieve our dreams.

Self-doubt can be especially insidious because it can creep in at any stage of the journey, even when we have already achieved some level of success. It can also be fueled by external factors such as criticism or rejection.

One way to combat self-doubt is to develop a strong sense of self-awareness. This means being able to recognize and acknowledge our own strengths and weaknesses, as well as our unique qualities and talents. By focusing on our strengths and building upon them, we can develop a sense of confidence and self-assurance.

Another strategy is to set achievable goals and celebrate small wins along the way. This can help to build momentum and keep us motivated, even when we encounter setbacks or challenges.

It can also be helpful to seek out feedback and constructive criticism from trusted mentors or colleagues. This can provide valuable insights and help us to identify areas for improvement, without reinforcing negative self-talk.

Finally, it is important to practice self-compassion and treat ourselves with kindness and understanding, even when we make mistakes or encounter setbacks. By cultivating a positive self-image and treating ourselves with the same compassion and understanding that we would offer to a friend, we can build resilience and overcome self-doubt.

In conclusion, self-doubt can be a significant obstacle on the journey towards our destiny. However, by developing self-awareness, setting achievable goals, seeking feedback, and practicing self-compassion, we can overcome this obstacle and achieve our full potential.

Chapter 18:
The Power of Community: Finding Support and Strength in Others

Throughout our lives, we will undoubtedly face challenges and obstacles that will test our limits and push us to our breaking points. In these moments, it can be easy to feel alone and isolated, as if we are the only ones struggling with our problems. However, this could not be further from the truth. In reality, there are countless people around us who are going through similar struggles and who can offer us support and encouragement when we need it most.

In this chapter, we will explore the power of community and how it can help us to overcome obstacles in our lives. We will discuss the importance of seeking out a support network, whether it be through family, friends, or other groups and organizations. We will also examine the benefits of giving back to our communities and helping others in need, as this can not only provide us with a sense of purpose and fulfillment but can also strengthen our own resilience and coping abilities.

One of the key benefits of being part of a community is the sense of belonging and connectedness it can provide. When we are surrounded by people who share our values, interests, and experiences, we feel a sense of camaraderie and support that can help us to weather even the toughest storms. This is why it is so important to seek out communities that resonate with us, whether it be a religious organization, a volunteer group, or a support group for a particular issue or challenge.

In addition to finding support, giving back to our communities can also be a powerful way to build resilience and strength. When we help others in need, we not only provide a valuable service, but we also build our own sense of purpose and meaning in life. This can help us to reframe our own struggles in a more positive light and give us the motivation we need to keep going, even when things seem bleak.

Ultimately, the power of community lies in its ability to provide us with the support, encouragement, and motivation we need to overcome obstacles and live our best lives. Whether we are going through a tough time or simply seeking to build more meaning and purpose in our lives, there is no substitute for the strength and resilience that comes from being part of a caring and supportive community.